WORKBOOK

For

What Happened To You?

Conversation on Trauma, Resilience and Healing

GuideQuest Reads

Copyright © 2024 GuideQuest Reads
All right reserved
No part of this book may be reproduced or transmitted in any form or by any means, electronic or mechanical, including photocopying, recording or by any information storage and retrieval system, without written permission from the author

Disclaimer

This workbook is an unofficial companion to the original book. It is not endorsed, sponsored, or associated with the original author, or publisher of the original book. All views and opinions expressed in this workbook are those of the author and do not necessarily reflect the views and opinions of the author or publisher of the original book

How To Use This Workbook

Welcome, daring self-discovery explorers! This section serves as your compass, guide, and key to accessing the transformational possibilities contained inside the pages of this workbook.

Begin by locating a peaceful, comfortable place where you can focus on your ideas without being distracted. This workbook is your personal sanctuary, so treat it as a sacred commitment to your own development.

Each activity should be approached with an open heart and mind. Allow Dr. Perry's and Oprah's comments to reverberate within you, and allow the contemplative exercises to function as mirrors reflecting the depth of your own.

Authenticity is essential in this workbook. Don't be afraid to express the nuances of your feelings or the complexities of your experiences. Sincere reflection is the compass that will lead you to significant realizations.

Each completed task (which includes thoughts provoking exercises, journals, worksheets and proposed strategies) represents a step forward in your path. Celebrate your progress and the fortitude it takes to go into the depths of your own story.

Consider sharing your discoveries with friends, family, or other readers. Conversations about your findings might help you comprehend them better and build a supportive community around your personal improvement.

Remember, this workbook is a compass directing you towards self-discovery and empowerment, not a destination. Accept the trip, embrace the disclosures, and have faith that it will leave an everlasting impact on your road to personal development.

Are you ready to realize your full potential? The adventure has begun. Have fun exploring!

4

Table of Contents

Statement of Intent — 7
Introduction — 8

Chapter 1: Making Sense of the World — 9
Summary of the Chapter — 9
Transformative Exercises — 10
Proposed Strategies — 11

Chapter 2: Seeking Balance — 27
Summary of the Chapter. — 27
Transformative Exercises. — 28
Proposed Strategies. . — 30
Self-evaluation. — 32

Chapter 3: How We Were Loved — 33
Summary of the Chapter — 33
Transformative Exercises — 34
Proposed Strategies — 37
Self-evaluation. — 38

Chapter 4: The Spectrum of Trauma — 39
Summary of the Chapter. — 39
Transformative Exercises — 40
Proposed Strategies. — 43
Self-evaluation. — 45

Chapter 5: Connecting the Dots — 46
Summary of the Chapter. — 46
Transformative Exercises — 47
Proposed Strategies — 49
Self-evaluation — 54

Chapter 6: From Coping to Healing — 55
Summary of the Chapter — 55
Transformative Exercises — 56
Proposed Strategies — 58
Self-evaluation — 60

Chapter 7: Post-Traumatic Wisdom	61
Summary of the Chapter	61
Transformative Exercises	62
Proposed Strategies	64
Self-evaluation	66
Chapter 8: Our Brains, Our Biases, Our Systems	67
Summary of the Chapter	67
Transformative Exercises	68
Proposed Strategies	69
Self-evaluation	70
Chapter 9: Rational Hunger in the Modern World	71
Summary of the Chapter	71
Transformative Exercises	72
Proposed Strategies	74
Self-evaluation	75
Chapter 10: What We Need Now	75
Summary of the Chapter	75
Transformative Exercises	76
Proposed Strategies	77
Self-evaluation	79

Statement of Intent

I,_____, earnestly commit to the transformative journey indicated in this workbook.

This commitment is an act of self-care, self-empowerment, and an investment in my overall well-being.

By signing below, I commit to approach each exercise with an open heart and mind, welcoming the process and allowing the transforming potential of this workbook to develop within me.

Signature _____

Date _____

Introduction

This workbook brings the practicability of Dr. Bruce and Oprah Winfrey discussion into light. To enable you internalize the lesson learnt from their main book through presentation of thought provoking exercises, journals, worksheets, self-evaluation proposed strategies to heal from traumatic experiences.

A brief introduction of the main book;
The main book was co written by Oprah Winfrey and Dr. Bruce Perry, describes Oprah's horrible childhood memories, including repeated beatings from her grandmother. The maltreatment, which was considered the norm in rural America, caused severe emotional scars, encouraging a lifetime habit of conditioned obedience and people-pleasing. The narrative highlights the significant influence of early trauma on shaping individuals, documenting Oprah's journey from abuse to resilience. It also shows Dr. Perry's significance in Oprah's life, their partnership on child abuse, and their shared dedication to researching the consequences of trauma on brain development. The book, titled "What Happened to You?" investigates the transforming effect of asking, "What happened to you?" as a basic inquiry, rather than "What's wrong with you?" in order to encourage knowledge and empathy for the events that define people's lives.

Chapter 1 :Making Sense of The World

Summary of the Chapter

Oprah Winfrey and Dr. Bruce Perry co-wrote the tale, which details Oprah's traumatic childhood recollections, including frequent beatings by her grandmother. Maltreatment was considered the norm in rural America, and it left deep emotional scars, fostering a lifetime habit of conditioned obedience and people-pleasing.

The story emphasizes the importance of early trauma in shaping humans, following Oprah's journey from abuse to resilience.

It also demonstrates Dr. Perry's importance in Oprah's life, their collaboration on child abuse, and their shared commitment to investigating the effects of trauma on brain development. "What Happened to You?" studies the transformational impact of asking "What happened to you?" as a fundamental inquiry rather than "What's wrong with you?" in order to develop understanding and empathy for the events that shape people's life.

To identify if you are affected by trauma or not, this thought provoking question is necessary to be answered by you faithfully.

> **Are there recurring, powerful emotional reactions or behavioral patterns in your life that appear disproportionate to the current circumstance, and do they frequently come from earlier events, suggesting a potential influence of trauma?**

___
___
___
___
___
___
___
___
___
___
___
___
___
___

If you have identify some of these disproportionate or past experiences evoking potential impact of trauma, the next thing is to determine the sources of such trauma, the next question will help you achieve this

> **Are there certain memories or incidents in your past that continually elicit strong emotional responses or discomfort, suggesting that they may be sources of trauma impacting your current experiences?**

_____

_____

_____

_____

_____

_____

_____

_____

_____

_____

_____

_____

_____

_____

Do you see repeated patterns of conflict, trust concerns, or difficulties in building deep connections in your relationships? Could these patterns be related to prior experiences that could be possible causes of trauma influencing your current relationships?

The next question is to investigate further if the trauma is from your childhood? if your answer to this is Yes; then answer the following question with all sincerity and purpose that you want to overcome this trauma; if the two questions is peculiar to your case answer the two but if otherwise choose one and provide your detailed answer

Can you recall any times in your childhood when you were subjected to physical, emotional, or verbal abuse, maybe at the hands of caregivers or others, which resulted in emotions of dread, embarrassment, or anguish, suggesting probable indicators of childhood abuse?

> Can you identify how your parents' divorce or separation, as well as how it was conveyed to you, may have affected emotions of abandonment, bewilderment, or instability, affecting your sense of security, trust in relationships, or knowledge of family dynamics?

___
___
___
___
___
___
___
___
___
___
___
___
___
___
___
___

After the preceding question, the next question you write down is the effect this trauma has had on your brain and in the way you behave (behavior)

Do you have heightened stress reactions, such as increased anxiety, intrusive thoughts, or difficulties concentrating, which may reflect the impact of trauma on the functioning of your brain?

Have you seen any persistent patterns of avoidance, trouble building and sustaining relationships, or difficulties regulating emotions, indicating probable behavioral repercussions from traumatic experiences in the past?

After knowing the effect of trauma on your brain and in your behavior, its pertinent to strategies on ways of overcoming such trauma. This two powerful strategies will help you achieve that if followed carefully and taking seriously

As a daily practice, investigate mindfulness and relaxation approaches. Can you commit to adding activities like deep breathing, meditation, or grounding exercises into your daily routine to assist relax your nervous system and encourage brain recovery after trauma?

_____
_____
_____
_____
_____
_____
_____
_____
_____
_____
_____
_____
_____
_____

SIMPLE MINDFULNESS PRACTICES

Breathe deeply and slowly

Sit still and close your eyes

Be present in the moment, here and now

Think of 3 things you're grateful for

Set aside 5-10 minutes to meditate

> Seek the help of a mental health professional to help you build good coping mechanisms and communication methods. As part of your recovery path, are you open to learning and applying new ways of responding to stress, relationships, and obstacles, creating beneficial behavioral changes?

It very important to investigate how trauma influence your future behaviors and relationship

> How do prior traumatic events impact your expectations, anxieties, or decision-making processes when imagining your future while contemplating your present objectives and aspirations? Can you pinpoint how these variables impact your future behavior?

How have prior traumas influenced your capacity to trust, communicate, and connect with people, when you reflect on your patterns in creating and sustaining relationships? What particular impacts can you identify from prior traumas, and how do they impact your present and future relationships?

Will we now dive into overcoming trauma influence on your future and also in your relationship

> **Consider imagining a future that is not primarily defined by previous tragedies. How can you actively develop and pursue objectives that are true to yourself, free of the limits of prior experiences? What measures can you take to foster beneficial behaviors that promote your health and personal development?**

_____

_____

_____

_____

_____

_____

_____

_____

_____

_____

_____

_____

_____

_____

_____

> Consider the characteristics you seek in healthy partnerships. How can you try to actively develop trust, improve communication, and foster partnerships that reflect your values? What measures can you take to overcome the impact of prior traumas and form connections that benefit your general well-being?

NOTE :- This strategy is a gradual and personalized process. What we will not tell you is its a fast process! No it's not. But this is a right step to your healing process! This we can boldly say

Mindfulness Practices: Make mindfulness a part of your everyday routine. Meditation, deep breathing, and grounding techniques can all help you stay present and manage your worry about the future.

> Goal Setting and Visualization: For your future, set realistic and empowering objectives. Imagine the life you wish to live, free of past tragedies. Divide your objectives into reasonable chunks and celebrate minor triumphs along the way.

Set Goals
- ☐ _____

Objectives
- ☐ _____
- ☐ _____
- ☐ _____
- ☐ _____

Write on how you will love to celebrate each achieved objectives

1 _____

2 _____

3 _____

4 _____

Proposed Strategies

- Self-Compassion and Forgiveness: Practice self-compassion and forgiveness. Recognize that your history does not define you, and it is OK to make errors or confront problems. Treat yourself with the same compassion and understanding that you would provide to a friend.

- Building Communication abilities: Learn and practice good communication abilities. Building and sustaining successful relationships requires open and honest communication. Learn to express your wants and feelings while actively listening to others.

- Setting limits: In your relationships, set clear and healthy limits. Recognize your own limitations and assertively discuss them. Boundaries must be set and respected in order to ensure balance and well-being.

- Creating a Support Network: Create a supporting network of friends and loved ones. Healthy connections with a solid support system may give empathy, encouragement, and a feeling of belonging, all of which can help to mitigate the harmful consequences of prior traumas.

Chapter 2 : Seeking Balance

Summary of the Chapter

The plot explores the connection between the heart, rhythm, and regulation, and how early childhood experiences impact self-regulation.

It highlights the importance of early caregiving and stress-response systems, and the long-term impact of stress on the human body.

Dr. Bruce Perry discusses the link between trauma and addiction, emphasizing the need to tackle addiction from a trauma-aware perspective, understanding the underlying processes, and recognizing the value of relational incentives in combating addictive behaviors.

> Consider your early life experiences. Is there anything that comes to mind? Write it down with utmost sincerity?

Have you pondered on your early life experiences? How do you think they may have influenced your stress-response mechanisms? Is there any evidence of developmental trauma influencing your current state of well-being?

Can you recall specific childhood events or patterns of contact with caregivers that may have affected your capacity to self-regulate emotions and behaviors when you reflect on your early life experiences? How do you think these early events have influenced your present coping mechanisms for stress, frustration, or other emotional states?

How do you survive in times of adversity? Are there any harmful habits, such as substance abuse or binge eating?

Proposed Strategies

- Take care of your nutrition, sleep, and hydration. A well-balanced lifestyle has a substantial impact on emotional well-being.

- Divide your work into smaller, more attainable objectives. This can assist in avoiding feelings of overload and frustration.

- Organise your tasks and prioritise them according to their significance. This can help you focus on one issue at a time and lessen stress.

- Be kind with yourself. Recognise that everyone encounters difficulties, and that making mistakes is normal. Treat yourself with the same kindness you would show a friend.

- Manage your time effectively by prioritising work and avoiding procrastination. This can assist alleviate the stress and strain associated with deadlines.

- Accept that you do not have complete control over everything. Let go of what is beyond your control and concentrate on what you can affect.

- Surround yourself with people who are encouraging and upbeat. Share your experiences and views with trustworthy friends and family members.

- Participate in things that offer you joy and laughter. Laughter is an excellent stress reliever.

Chapter 3: How We Were Loved

Summary of the Chapter

The chapter discussed Gloria, a traumatic mother, and her daughter Tilly, who are placed under foster care by Mama P.

Dr. Perry observes their relationship and the positive changes they have made. The chapter emphasizes the impact of early life experiences on an individual's development and the importance of love and connection.

It also discusses the neuroscience of stress responses and the role of the brain's adaptability in trauma recovery. The chapter also highlights the healing power of connection and hope.

Examine any painful events from your history. What effect have they had on your stress-response systems and coping mechanisms?

Consider your early life experiences and look for instances of love and connection. How have these experiences influenced your present emotional well-being?

Consider good changes or personal progress in your life. What role did hopeful partnerships and supportive relationships play in these transformations?

> Consider the simple, daily occurrences in your life that made you feel connected. How can you include more of these moments in your regular life?

Self-evaluation

When I _____my early life experiences, I uncovered important moments of _____that had a huge impact on my _____.

Recognizing the _____ influence of these events on my _____ self has increased my _____ of the enduring significance of early _____.

Chapter 4: The Spectrum of Trauma

Summary of the Chapter

Oprah and Dr. Perry examine the impact of trauma, highlighting its complexities and the importance of understanding. They explore the ACE research and its relationship to adult health difficulties.

To comprehend trauma's layers, Perry highlights the significance of taking a "What happened to you?" approach. He also discusses the ACE score's limits in comprehending an individual's trauma path.

He also highlights the need for therapeutic doses and short, good caring contacts. Despite the hurdles, the chapter concludes that trauma recovery is feasible, and that early intervention can have a substantial influence on resilience-building.

Examine the extent and strength of your ties to family, community, and culture. How have these connections affected your mental health? Consider both good and negative factors.

> Consider the timing of adversity in your life. How do you think the timing has affected your present mental health? Consider the first several months of life and the succeeding developmental phases

Recall instances of brief yet beneficial caring exchanges in your life. How did these events make you feel? Investigate the influence of such occasions on your well-being.

Consider times when you may have experienced dissociative reactions to stress. How did your mind and body react? Consider the triggers and their influence on your general well-being.

Self-evaluation

As I go on a road of _____,
I've had profound thoughts inspired by Oprah and Dr. Perry's informative chat. To gauge my progress, I diligently responded to _____ concrete questions targeted at implementing the _____ from their talk to my own life.

This self-evaluation acts as a compass, directing me toward a better understanding of my _____

I found moments of emotional resonance and revelation as I dived into recognizing and meditating on my early hardships.

Recognizing these _____has been both _____.
My increasing knowledge of how previous experiences impact my current narrative demonstrates progress.

Think about a recent positive caring contact in your life. Describe the specifics, emotions, and any insights obtained from this experience. Examine how such encounters affect your emotional control and well-being.

Chapter 5: Connecting the Dots

Summary of the Chapter

Oprah and Dr. Perry talk about the impact of trauma on individuals and societies, dating it back to terrible childhood events. They talk about transgenerational transmission, the biological and societal elements of inherited behaviors, and the significance of deliberate change in breaking negative cycles.

They also talk about the intergenerational effects of trauma on mental and physical health, highlighting the significance of recognizing one's past in order to address one's current well-being.

In addition, the chapter explores the sequential nature of brain processing and its influence on communication and reasoning, highlighting the necessity of emotional management and connection in reaching logical thought.

Reflect on your own family history and consider if there are patterns of behavior or emotional traits that have been passed down through generations.

Reflect on a positive belief or value you received from your family or community. How can you consciously pass on this positive trait to future generations?

Explore potential physical symptoms you may be experiencing and reflect on whether there could be a connection to past traumatic experiences

> Identify any negative beliefs or biases you've observed in your family or community. Consider how these may impact your worldview and interactions with others.

Engage in conversations with family members about shared experiences and consider how these may have influenced your worldview

> Consider the diversity in your social circle and daily interactions. How can you celebrate differences and promote inclusivity in your immediate environment?

> Evaluate the media, institutions, and communities you engage with. Are there elements of bias or negativity present? How can you intentionally expose yourself to more positive influences?

Self-evaluation

Reflecting on my family history, I notice
_____
that have been passed down through generations.

Understanding these patterns enables me to
_____
_____
on my own behaviors and emotions.

I recollect a childhood experience that may have affected my current worries or anxiety. By reflecting on this event, I was able to
_____
_____
_____
_____

Chapter 6: From Coping to Healing

Summary of the Chapter

Dr. Bruce Perry describes how early relationship interactions shape brain development and general well-being. He tells the narrative of Thomas and James, two brothers who had diverse behaviors as a result of their early childhood experiences. Perry highlights the need of continuous, predictable interactions during infancy, as well as the negative impacts of neglect.

He also explores the neurobiological effects of dismissive interactions on newborns, which leads to emotional hunger and a need to belong. The notion of dissociation is investigated, emphasizing its adaptive character but potential for harmful misuse.

The discussion also delves into the complexities of abusive relationships and the brain's malleability throughout life. Recognizing and breaking patterns is critical for assisting traumatized persons in developing better worldviews.

Consider a specific childhood memory in which you felt supported and controlled, or ignored and dysregulated. Consider how the emotions linked with that recollection may have impacted your present opinions and behaviors.

> Examine your existing relationships. Are there consistent and supportive patterns, or do you see chaotic or neglecting elements? What effect may this have on your well-being?

Worksheet on Neglect

1. Describe a specific case of neglect in your life.
2. When was the neglect committed?
3. What was the neglecting pattern?
4. How serious was the neglect?
5. How long was it?
6. Were any buffering elements present throughout the period of neglect?
7. Consider how neglect affects different elements of development.
8. How does neglect affect emotional well-being and social interactions?
9. Did neglect impact learning capacity and cognitive functioning?
10. Was there any visible influence on physical health and motor skills?
11. Consider the presence of splintered or fractured neglect.
12. How chaotic or unorganized was the neglect?
13. Can you name particular development domains that were overlooked while others were not?
14. Investigate the similarities between neglect and trauma.

Proposed Strategies

- Practice self-compassion and forgiveness. Recognize that your history does not define you, and it is OK to make errors or confront problems. Treat yourself with the same compassion and understanding that you would provide to a friend.

- Create a supporting network of friends and loved ones. Healthy connections with a solid support system may give empathy, encouragement, and a feeling of belonging, all of which can help to mitigate the harmful consequences of prior traumas.

- To heal and grow from trauma, prioritize building healthy relationships, engaging in therapeutic interventions, practicing mindfulness and self-regulation, engaging in narrative therapy, using expressive arts, and engaging in education about trauma.

- Develop self-compassion, challenge self-blame, and practice self-care routines. Connect with community organizations and support groups to learn from others and advocate for trauma-informed policies. Prioritize regular exercise, a balanced diet, and sufficient sleep for overall well-being.

Self-evaluation

When I recall a certain childhood experience, I recall feeling supported and in charge. The emotions associated _____ shaped my current beliefs and habits.

Recognizing the significance of this memory assists me to better understand my need
_____
_____

When I examine my existing connections, I notice patterns _____, as well as components that are chaotic or neglectful. Because it adds flexibility in the degree of emotional support and stability I feel in my relationships, this combination of dynamics can have _____

Chapter 7: Post-traumatic Wisdom

Summary of the Chapter

Dr. Perry and Oprah debate the notion of resilience in children, contending that they are adaptable rather than naturally resilient.

They emphasize the relevance of connectivity and support in developing resilience, as well as the function of a sensitive stress-response system in those who have been exposed to chronic stress or trauma.

They also talk about how relationships may heal and the importance of social ties in developing resilience and post-traumatic knowledge. They also talk on the value of healing groups and the negative effects of social isolation on mental and physical health.

The discussion finishes with a plea for the formation of supportive networks to assist individuals in navigating trauma and developing resilience.

Consider a time in your life when you failed. Describe your emotional reaction, the assistance you got, and the final result. Consider how this incident influenced your own development and resilience.

Describe a time when you were heard and supported by someone at a difficult period. Consider the aspects of the connection and how comparable assistance may be provided to others in need.

> Describe a time when you experienced the good influence of community support, whether it was at a difficult period or a time of joy. Consider how this assistance improved your well-being and sense of belonging.

Journal Entry

Instruction : Visit a neighborhood community gathering and fill the following reflective activity

Today, I went to a neighborhood community gathering where I met neighbors and talked about our common _____

The sense of belonging and support was _____, and it reminded me how important it is to create and nurture community _____

The different contacts soothed and cheered me, and I saw the _____ for developing a helpful network.

Moving ahead, I intend to investigate new community initiatives and offer my _____ to the promotion of relational diversity.

Self-evaluation

When I think back on a moment when I failed, I remember feeling a mix of
_____

The aid I got during this trying time was critical to my _____

Mentors and friends encouraged me to endure and learn from failures by helping me realize
_____

Finally, this experience not only enhanced my resilience but also considerably aided my
_____

I now see failure as a stepping stone to achievement, knowing that setbacks are chances for _____ and _____

Chapter 8: Our Brains, Our Biases, Our Systems

Summary of the Chapter

Oprah and Dr. Perry talk about Shaka Senghor, a man who converted after serving 19 years in jail for second-degree murder.

They talk on the necessity of identifying and resolving trauma, the difficulties that people like Shaka experience within society structures, and the concept of trauma-informed treatment (TIC).

They also examine the impact of trauma on children's education, highlighting the importance of trauma-aware schools and tailored mental health treatments.

They also talk about the brain's response to stress, implicit prejudice, and racism, highlighting the need of dealing with these issues via real-life experiences and relationships.

Dr. Perry is optimistic about good change via trauma-informed education and the development of linked communities.

Consider a personal scenario in which you encountered difficulties in the school system. Investigate how underlying stress or trauma may have affected these difficulties. Consider what type of assistance or improvements in the instructional method may have improved your experience.

Consider a moment in which you were aware of your unconscious prejudice. Describe your feelings and ideas as they emerged. Consider how this understanding might be used to motivate you to improve your attitudes and behaviors. Write about one practical move you may take to confront and change your prejudices.

Self-evaluation

Reflecting on a personal scenario involving school system issues, I see the impact of underlying stress or trauma on these obstacles. The demands and emotional toll of unsolved issues hampered my capacity to efficiently navigate the school environment.

In retrospect, _____ method may have mitigated the impact of underlying stress, perhaps improving my whole school experience. This realization emphasizes the need of detecting and managing emotional well-being in educational environments for optimal _____

Remembering a time when I became aware of my unconscious bias was both _____. The appearance of biased thinking elicited emotions of _____ and the understanding that there were components of my attitude that needed to be examined.

This understanding _____ me to change my thoughts and _____. One practical step toward confronting and changing my preconceptions is to actively seek out various viewpoints through _____ and _____. I hope to confront and alter established prejudices by deliberately exposing myself to diverse points of view, promoting _____.

70

Chapter 9: Rational Hunger in the Modern World

Summary of the Chapter

Dr. Perry discusses his experience with Māori healers in New Zealand and the importance of community-focused trauma healing.

He highlights the role of whanaungatanga, reciprocal relationships, and family connection in Māori healing. The chapter also discusses the decline in empathy due to screen-based technologies and the rise in anxiety, depression, and suicide.

Dr. Perry highlights the importance of connectedness and the potential for isolation as a new form of trauma. The chapter concludes with discussions on touch, screen time, and "techno-hygiene" rules.

Describe a recent interaction with someone with whom you felt a true connection. What made it significant? Consider how these relationships affect your general well-being.

Consider a time in your life when you had a strong feeling of belonging and connection. Describe the situation, the persons involved, and the feelings you felt. Investigate how this sense of connection contributed to your well-being and whether comparable experiences might be recreated or enhanced.

Self-evaluation

When I interacted with _____, a recent interaction that struck out as an important moment happened. This connection was distinguished by genuine communication, mutual understanding, and a feeling of shared purpose.

The intimate relationship formed via similar ideals and open communication was what made it noteworthy. This form of relationship has a significant influence _____, providing emotional support, lessening feelings of _____and contributing to an overall good a _____

These significant relationships are _____ to my mental and emotional wellness. They remind me of the value of creating and cherishing connections that provide true connection, so improving my _____

Chapter 10: What We Need Now

Summary of the Chapter

The chapter delves into Oprah Winfrey's own experiences with trauma and its consequences, as well as the possibility of healing through a trauma-informed approach.

It also emphasizes the necessity of understanding the brain's response to trauma, with a focus on empathy and post-traumatic wisdom.

The chapter advocates for increased societal awareness as well as trauma-informed communities.

Consider a difficult experience from your past. How has this event influenced your ideas, behaviors, and interpersonal relationships? What insights or lessons have you acquired from this experience, and how has it aided your personal development?

Have you ever asked a close friend or family member, "What happened to you?" in a compassionate and understanding manner? How did this exchange strengthen your bond or foster greater understanding?

How can you actively contribute to the development of a trauma-informed community? Is there anything particular you can do in terms of conversations, seminars, or campaigning to encourage trauma-aware behaviors in various settings?

Self-evaluation

The insights and lessons derived from this challenging experience have played a crucial role in my personal _____

It served as a catalyst for _____, pushing me to embrace discomfort as a natural part of the journey toward _____

I've learned to view setbacks as opportunities for _____, shaping a more positive and adaptable mindset.

Ultimately, this challenging _____ has contributed significantly to my _____, fostering a sense of strength, empathy, and wisdom that continues to guide my journey.

Made in the USA
Las Vegas, NV
30 June 2025